FREE to THINK

Free to Think
The truth shall set you free

James Jones
Senior Pastor of Divergent Church of God

Xulon Press

Xulon Press
2301 Lucien Way #415
Maitland, FL 32751
407.339.4217
www.xulonpress.com

© 2018 by James Jones

All rights reserved solely by the author. The author guarantees all contents are original and do not infringe upon the legal rights of any other person or work. No part of this book may be reproduced in any form without the permission of the author. The views expressed in this book are not necessarily those of the publisher.

Scripture quotations taken from the Holy Bible, New International Version (NIV). Copyright © 1973, 1978, 1984, 2011 by Biblica, Inc.™. Used by permission. All rights reserved.

Scripture quotations taken from the New King James Version (NKJV). Copyright © 1982 by Thomas Nelson, Inc. Used by permission. All rights reserved.

Printed in the United States of America.

ISBN-13: 9781545629307

Table of Contents

Introduction ix
Chapter 1: The Standard 1
Chapter 2: The Standard Part 2 9
Chapter 3: Our Origins 19
Chapter 4: This Is No Culture War 29
Chapter 5: The Moral Compass 41
Chapter 6: The New Moral Compass 51
Chapter 7: The Truth About Love 55
Chapter 8: We Are as Close to God as
    We Want to Be 65

Introduction

I have found in life that sometimes the simplest answers can be the best answers. For example, what happens when an irresistible force meets an immovable object? The answer is so simple that we tend to miss it, but I will come back to that in a minute. So many of the "truths" we hold to in our lives are not actually based on truth at all. Often they are based on the opinion of someone else. Sometimes we don't even realize this because oftentimes opinions are taught as though they are observable truths when in actuality they are not.

Another thing I have noticed is people sometimes have a tendency to complicate things more than they need to be. Perhaps it makes us feel a little better about who we are, if we can give a complex answer to a simple question. When I was younger we would visit my grandmother. In her apartment she had a plaque that said, "If you can't dazzle them with brilliance, then baffle them with doubletalk." Actually it used a more colorful metaphor than doubletalk, but I think you get the picture.

So together we are going to look at quite a few things as we venture through the pages of this book. While we will look for answers, what we really want to do is set you free to think. I am not going to try to answer every question there is out there, but I will answer a few—hopefully just enough to get you ready to search for truth yourself and not just trust what you have been told.

So about that impossible question we started out with? What does happen when an irresistible force meets an immovable object? We find out which one is what it says it is. There is really nothing else that can happen in that situation. Just because we label something as immovable does not mean we have all of the evidence. In like manner, if we label something irresistible, that does not make it so if we have not observed that to be absolutely true. So when two things we have labeled come into contact in such a way, we have to be open enough to realize we may not have all the answers yet. We need to be open enough to realize that even though something carries a label, until it has been put to the test, we may not really know what it is. That is what it means to be free to think.

Chapter 1
The Standard

Can we live a life that is based on an absolute truth? Can we really determine what is right and what is wrong? What if doing something wrong brings a good result? Wouldn't that then make it a good choice, even if it was the wrong thing to do?

In a world where we are seeing more and more of the ideology "the ends justifies the means," it would not be too much of a reach to say that anything goes so long as there is a positive outcome. That said, deep down I think we still desire to see moral truth. I think it can be evidenced that we want to see the right thing done. Take the following story for example:

> A young man named Joey worked at a Dairy Queen in his town. One day at Joey's Dairy Queen, a man who was blind placed his order, and while paying for the order he accidentally dropped a twenty-dollar

bill. The lady behind him in line quickly grabbed the twenty-dollar bill from the ground and held on to it. She didn't realize that Joey and another customer had seen what happened. Joey confronted her quietly about the incident, encouraging her to do the right thing and return the money, but she insisted it was her twenty-dollar bill. Joey then firmly insisted she do the right thing, and when she refused, he refused to serve her. Before she left, she loudly berated Joey in front of everyone and left the establishment displaying great anger and fury. Joey then walked over to the blind man, who was now seated at a table in the dining area and completely unaware of what had just happened. Joey then reached into his own pocket, pulled out a twenty-dollar bill, and handed it to the blind man. He said, "Here, sir, you dropped this twenty-dollar bill, and I just wanted to make sure you get it back."

 The blind man, not knowing everything that had just happened, was grateful. Another customer saw this entire scene unfold, and she sent an email to the company about this noble teenager who had just done something so wonderful. The store then posted a copy of the email with a picture of Joey beside it. The story soon went viral, and Joey received calls, accolades, and attention from the local newspapers, and even television interviews.

So why was this so heralded? What seemed like the right thing to do, what seemed like a good deed, was then celebrated with great fanfare and attention from every direction. It is an example of how people still love a feel-good story, but even more than that, how we respond when we see the right thing done.

We live in a day when qualities such as integrity and truth are not as prevalent as they once were. Educators rewrite history to fit the modern objectives. Scientists falsify data to advance their own theories. In media, journalism, and even government, we are given partial truths so that we will hear what we are "supposed" to hear. We are witnessing those in power or influence model the idea that it is more important to accomplish what we feel needs to be done than to be honest and upright. There is even an advertisement in a popular magazine for a face cream that says it will make you look like you were Photoshopped, and the model in the ad is Photoshopped. This is the world we live in.

You see, in a society where we are being almost indoctrinated that the ends justifies the means, there is still that part inside of us that knows better—that element inside each of us that desires more, that desires truth. The truth is it does matter how you get there; the journey is just as important as the destination. When we begin to receive that as a matter of principal, we are ready to consider that there is right and wrong. We are ready to consider that there is truth that is absolute, and if there is, we are ready to consider what would be the standard that truth is measured against. It would have to be something quite unique to be the source of absolute truth, something timeless and built on something deeper than just natural understanding. The standard I am speaking of is the Bible, the words from God Himself.

I take the stand that all truth is from God, that all life is from God, and therefore all truth is spiritual in nature because it finds its origin in God. All life is also spiritual in nature, as we are created with an eternal spirit given by God. Therefore that spirit within us is what so desperately longs for the truth and the standards of God. Thus the reaction we saw in the story we just read about Joey the teenager who worked at Dairy Queen. Deep down we know there is more, and until we reach for it, we will find ourselves attempting to reach for anything that can bring personal peace. We will only find that peace and fulfillment we desire in our spirit in the truth that is from God.

As we look in the Bible, in John 8:31-47, Jesus is speaking of spiritual truth. I encourage you to take the time to read this text when you can; it will be enlightening as we venture together through the pages of this book. In this text, He is expounding on truth to a group of listeners, but they are unable to receive this truth. Jesus makes the great statement, "You shall know the truth, and the truth shall set you free." His listeners began to declare they were already free, that they were not slaves to anyone. The truth is they were unable to receive what he was saying because of spiritual blindness and the spiritual bondage they were in. They couldn't receive the truth because the truth is spiritually discerned, and they were bound to a spirit of lies from the father of lies, also called Satan.

To say such a thing as truth is spiritually discerned may not be received well across the board in this day and age, but it is no less true, even if it is not initially accepted. So the next natural step is to defend that statement and not simply argue an idea. You will find one of the biggest lies Satan tells society today is that we are at war over ideas and ideology. We will look at this in depth in chapter 4, but for now let us stay on task and explore the claim that all truth is spiritual in nature and therefore is spiritually discerned.

So how did we get the Bible? Isn't it just the stories of people from long ago? I heard someone once say, "I can't read the Bible; it just has too many errors in it." Yet of those who have said this, none have ever actually read the Bible, which begs the question, "How do you know it is full of errors?" The answer is almost always because that's what they heard from someone else or that's what this teacher or that professor said.

Let's pause here for a moment. This book that you are reading right now has a purpose. The purpose is not so you can say, "Well, that's what James Jones said." The purpose of this book is so that you will begin to look at things objectively, so that you will find the truth and then be free to think without having to cling to what someone has told you. A true researcher finds truth. Let yourself become a researcher who examines the evidence. You will be liberated by what you find, I assure you of that.

So back to the Bible and how we received it and what it says within its pages. In 2 Peter 1:20–21, paraphrasing, Peter states that no prophecies recorded in Scripture came of the prophet's own interpretation or of their own thinking. Instead, they spoke as God enabled them, or as the Spirit of God carried them along to be exact. In 2 Timothy 3:16–17, Paul tells Timothy that all Scripture is God breathed. He says here that the Bible is inspired by God. What this means is while the writings came *through* men, the writings came *from* God. He is the source of truth, He is the source of the Bible, and while He chose people to write down this word and pass it along, He is the source of truth.

Truth is based on the fact that it is objective, not subjective. Therefore truth remains truth, even when it is inconvenient, even when it is the "hard way" of doing something. This is why there is a close relationship between the word *truth* and the word *integrity*, which means being steadfast, unchanging, and true to original form. We need truth in our lives, actions, and thoughts, and that will lead us to a life of integrity.

So we can understand the Bible is from God, but how do we understand what it says? How do we absorb and process the truth contained in the pages of the Bible. In the 1 Corinthians 2:10–14, Paul speaks to the church at Corinth about how we can receive truth from God. Paul shares how God connects with the believer and shares the "deep things" of Himself with them. We see that truth is indeed spiritual in nature; therefore it is spiritually discerned or comprehended. So as we follow God, He reveals not only Himself to us, but He also reveals His truth, His Word to us as well. This lends to what we discussed earlier when we looked at John 5, where Jesus was speaking to those around Him and they were unable to comprehend what He was saying. They completely missed it, and He told them it was because they had been blinded to the truth by Satan, the father of lies.

So many today say, "We are free," just like those in John 5 said to Jesus. The reason they say this so adamantly is because that is what they were told. It is not because they have looked for truth themselves but instead have just accepted what they have been told. Jesus told His listeners in John 5 that they were unable to receive truth because they did not belong to God. Instead they had been spiritually deceived into believing a false truth. Have you ever heard the expression "you wouldn't know it if it slapped you in the face"? Well, in this case Jesus didn't slap them in the face, but the truth was before them and being spoken to them, and they were unable to receive it because of a spiritual blindness.

Truth can be discovered, but it takes effort. It takes a desire to know the truth and not to "just be right." There is a standard for truth, and it is called the Bible. What is in the Bible are the very words of God, the creator of heaven and earth. The creator of all things, including all of our scientific laws that we have discovered along the way, has already given us His Word, which is truth. We need only to receive it into our spirit.

Chapter 2

The Standard Part 2

*T*he Bible is therefore the words of God and not of man. It is not from man's interpretation or even man's understanding but directly from God. So if we take that stand, can we also prove it is trustworthy in what it says? Can we be sure it has never been changed or altered from the original content? These are legitimate questions that should be asked if we are truly free to think. Again, the idea of this book is to encourage you to find truth for yourself and not just receive everything you are told by people regardless of their perceived intelligence or level of education.

So let's first look into its reliability as far as being unchanged and unaltered over the generations and how it came into existence. I have heard it said that the church gave us the Bible. In response I will say the church no more gave us the Bible than Sir Isaac Newton gave us gravity. Just as gravity was discovered as something that already existed, so the church put in order the writings that already existed.

By the year 180 AD, all four gospels were used widely throughout the entire church. By the year 230 AD, the New Testament books we read today had been accepted by the church as inspired literature. These books had to have eye-witness testimony and apostolic authorship to maintain a level of integrity to the content. We know these writings had to be in circulation within the generation that witnessed the events contained therein. So this tells us the information could be easily refuted, but there is not one instance where the information ever was challenged or refuted. The events did indeed take place, including the miracles of Jesus. Many tried to explain them away as magic, sorcery, or some strange events, but no one ever claimed that they did not happen.

One test for books of antiquity is to gauge their reliability by the number of manuscripts we have in existence today and how well they match the current copies in circulation. Another test is how much time has lapsed between the date of the existing manuscript and the events that are recorded therein. Take, for example, *The Annals of Rome*: the original was written around 119 AD. Today we have one manuscript that dates back to 850 AD, over 700 years later. That said, it is accepted across the board as an accurate historical document. The next example I offer you is *The*

Jewish War, by Josephus, written somewhere near the year 100 AD. We have almost 10 full manuscripts of this writing, dating back to the tenth century, almost 900 years after the original. Like with *The Annals of Rome*, it is also accepted as accurate and reliable. The next example we will look at is Homer's *Iliad*. It is most commonly accepted that this work was written near 800 BC. Today, we have 650 manuscripts that date back to between the second and third century AD, and obviously it is accepted as true to the original by most due to the number of manuscripts, even though they are almost 1,000 years removed from the original.

Those tests, when applied to these works of antiquity, seem to have settled most doubts about their authenticity and reliability, not to mention the integrity of their content when compared to the original. That said, what if we were to put the Bible to such a test? How would it fare. Well the truth is we have 24,000 manuscripts of the Bible that date back to the year 600 AD, less than 550 years from the events that are contained in its pages. That is a mountain of manuscripts when compared to 1, 10, or even 650. The Bible is also closer to the time of the events documented in its pages than any other of these works of antiquity. I feel like an infomercial host saying this, but wait, there's more! The 24,000 manuscripts we have are in 6 different languages, and all say the same thing as the Bible we hold today. Taking this into consideration, this means each of these translations obviously pulled from an earlier common root work.

I'm sorry I must say it one more time, are you ready, but wait, there's more. The Chester Beatty Biblical Papyri were discovered in 1930. They contain all 4 gospels, the book of Acts, 8 epistles from Paul, and the book of Hebrews. These manuscripts are dated back to the year 200 AD, just over 150 years after the actual events contained in the writings. Is the evidence getting overwhelming yet? Believe me when I say there is so much more than what I have shared with you out there waiting for you to discover it. There is no shortage of excellent books written by great researchers, and I encourage you to discover this truth and become free to think.

So what if we simply took accepted historical literature from sources like Josephus, Tacitus, Pliney the Lesser, and many others? We could establish many facts from the Bible. We could see that Jesus was born in Bethlehem, He had a following, and He did great signs and what some called sorcery. We can also find that He was sentenced to die by Pontius Pilate, died on a cross, there was an empty tomb, His followers would have rather died than deny Him, and He was worshiped as if He were a god. This is what we can collect from accepted historical writings from people who did not like Jesus or His followers. They were simply recording events that happened.

Here are a few interesting quotes about the Bible and its contents. F. F. Bruce, a professor at the University of Manchester, said, "There is no body of ancient literature in the world which enjoys such a wealth of good textual attestation as the New Testament." Sir Frederick Kenyon, the director of the British Museum, said, "In no other case is the interval of time between the composition of the book and the date of the earliest manuscripts so short as in that of the New Testament."

It is interesting that even with the overwhelming evidence, the Bible is still questioned and even denied as accurate by so many today. It serves to show us the argument is not academic because we can see it exceeds all other works of antiquity. It is not intellectual, either, because there is corroborating evidence through history that supports everything written therein. This brings us back to the heart of the matter: truth is spiritual in nature, and this battle to be able to think freely is not academic or intellectual. It is truly a spiritual battle.

We have focused more on the New Testament of the Bible and less on the Old Testament of the Bible, so let's take a look and see a few amazing things about the Old Testament of the Bible.

There are, of course, the prophecies of Jesus and His coming that were so detailed and also so accurate. I have heard it said that just from a statistical point of view, the chances of someone fulfilling just 8 of the well over 350 prophecies of Jesus would be the same as if we filled the entire state of Texas with quarters, randomly dropped in one red quarter, then blindfolded someone and had them walk through Texas for 8 days and then have them reach down and pull out the red quarter. The chances of them pulling out the red quarter would be the same as fulfilling just 8 of the over 350 prophecies concerning Jesus.

In Isaiah 44:28, Isaiah names Cyrus as the one who would say, "Let the temple in Jerusalem be rebuilt." You might say, "Well, that is not so interesting," and you would be correct. Where it gets interesting is the fact Isaiah said this 150 years before Cyrus was even born. Then Cyrus became the king of Persia and proclaimed that the Israelites could return from exile and rebuild the temple.

Sorry, I have to say it, are you ready, but wait, there's more! In Ezekiel 26, God says He will wipe out Tyre and scrape the remains into the sea and plunder all its wealth. It would be reduced to a place where people would drag fishing nets. God basically said, "I will turn your kingdom into a fishing hole."

Now the city of Tyre was very well fortified, with walls possibly 150 feet high and up to 15 feet thick. Just as God said, though, things went into motion when Nebuchadnezzar invaded Tyre 3 years after this prophecy. It took almost 13 years, but Nebuchadnezzar eventually broke down the walls and invaded the city, but he had been out smarted by the people of Tyre. They had moved the treasure and most of the people to a small island about half a mile off shore. Knowing Nebuchadnezzar had no navy to speak of, they were safe. Yes, the city was in ruins, but they fled with their treasures and lived. I know what you are thinking: that didn't happen the way God said it would. He said the walls would be torn down, the ruins would be scraped into the sea, and then everything they had would be taken away. You would be correct in saying that, but that is not the end of the story for Tyre, not yet. We now fast forward 250 years later as a military leader was taking land and advancing forward at all costs. This leader was Alexander the Great. He came to what was left of the city of Tyre and saw the settlement off the shore. He sent messengers to ask them for horses and supplies to help him on his way. The people of the city saw he had no navy and no ships, so they felt secure and said they would send him nothing. Infuriated, Alexander commanded his army to scrape the ruins of the former city into the sea. The walls used to be so massive that you can only imagine the amount of stone and debris that would have covered the ground. As they scraped all of that stone and debris into the sea, they made a bridge to cross to the island, where the army of Alexander the Great took over the city, killing 25,000 people and selling 30,000 into slavery and taking everything that was there. When this came to pass, it all happened exactly how God said it would.

In the search for truth, we see that God is indeed God, always knowing what is to come, even to the exact detail, and revealing it piece by piece to help us discover truth.

There are many other instances just like this. In the book of Nahum, God declares the destruction of Ninevah is coming, and several years later the Babylonians did just that. Perhaps no predictions are as attention grabbing as the prophecies of Daniel, which we can find in the book of Daniel. For generations skeptics said that the book of Daniel was a hoax. They declared that no one could possibly foretell events of the future with such detail. The consensus among nonbelievers was that the book had been written after these events and then worded to appear to be written beforehand. This was a valid argument they made. It would be unheard of to have such accuracy describing events that hadn't happened yet. It would therefore seem plausible that someone was trying to make this look like a book of prophecy when it was actually just a book of history. This was a prevailing theory until the discovery of many scrolls at a place called Qumran. Many scrolls were discovered, but Harvard University professor Frank M. Cross said the following about one of the scrolls: "One copy of Daniel is inscribed with the script from the second century BC; in some ways it is more striking than that of the oldest manuscripts from Qumran."

With so many texts recovered and amazing works of antiquity, why would he be so enamored with this one of the book of Daniel? I'm sure you have already guessed the reason, but if you didn't, it was because now we had a copy of the book of Daniel that predated the events that were prophesied in the book that supposedly had entirely too much detail for someone to foretell.

I want to hit pause again for a moment here. Remember, I am not trying to sell you on Christianity per se. My purpose is simply to set some facts before you so that you will consider the idea that maybe what you have always heard is not entirely accurate. In order to be free to think, you have to be willing to be wrong, even about conclusions you have come to. You also have to be willing to search and find out for yourself. There is so much more information about the Bible out there for you to explore. I have seen it, and guess what: I haven't "hung my hat" on what I already know. I am still looking today because I am free to think. I am free to consider every angle there is. That said, what I have found so far has convinced me of the accuracy and the authority of the Bible as God's words, which is why I hold to it as the standard for truth, for right and wrong, and for daily life. The small amount of information we covered in this chapter barely scratches the surface of the research that is available to the inquiring mind, but it should get you thinking at least, and that is the purpose of this book.

Chapter 3

Our Origins

Throughout this book I have made a few statements that may be called closeminded by some. While I have attempted to give you something to think about before you shoot down any thoughts in this book that you may have been told cannot be trusted, I am about to make another such statement. I make this statement not because someone has told me this—in fact, no one has ever said this to me. It is a conclusion I have come to by observing and researching. The statement is simply this: creation is the only viable explanation for our origin and the origin of the universe around us.

I know what you are thinking: that's a pretty confident statement, and I am truly confident about this. That said, we need look at this statement together and see what the facts around us point to.

Let's begin with a term we have all heard of before: the Big Bang, the theory that the universe, space, and mass were compressed and then released into existence through an explosion that caused the universe to grow and spread. Here are a few questions I never found an answer to. Where did the mass come from? Where did the space that the mass exploded into come from? The answers I found—answers such as it was always there, it just grew until it could no longer be held back—require a level of faith. Some would lean on Stephen Hawking's answer: the universe exists because it must. I understand that the man is a genius and has a level of knowledge few will ever attain in this world, so I say this with all respect: "it exists because it must" is the worst possible answer I could think of. The reason I say that is because it shuts down the ability to think. If you were to ask, "Why must it?" you would get the answer "it must." We deserve better answers than that.

We have looked at the Bible and what it says, and we can see the accuracy of so many things already. So let's take a look at what it has to say about our origins as well to see if we can extrapolate some understanding of the universe from the Bible.

The Bible says that God spoke creation into existence. This would say that creation came not gradually but all at one time, instantaneously. That would hold true to the first law of thermodynamics, which is the conservation of energy. That it came into being and maintains, or conserves from that start point. While the Big Bang theory would say that energy grew to a place of explosion, then energy and mass continued to grow for millions of years, this defies the first law of thermodynamics, the conservation of energy. Scientifically speaking, mass and energy do not grow, so why are we so willing to overlook this fact when we consider the Big Bang theory as more than a theory? Creation would make sense here in the fact that mass and energy do not grow, but instead they came into existence, and they maintain at the level that they came into existence.

From the Big Bang theory, we next would be led to the theory of evolution. Again there is a major challenge from the beginning of this theory. Much like with mass and energy in the big bang theory, life itself poses a challenge to evolution. Life doesn't come from non-life. The term *abiogenesis* is the concept that life can come from non-life, but this cannot happen. So the question remains, if you are going to say life progressed or evolved into what we see today, where did it start?

In the book *Evolution in Art*, author Alfred C. Hadden said, "[T]he belief in abiogenesis, or spontaneous generation as now taking place has completely disappeared from biological teaching." Why would he say this? Because it cannot happen. Yet if you turn to a source such as Wikipedia, it is stated to be science, something that has been seen, yet this is inaccurate.

The Miller–Urey experiment in 1952 was a breakthrough for the evolution theory. It was said they were able to create life from non-life, thus proving abiogenesis is possible. Their findings were published as the ability to create organic material from inorganic material, and they did, but if you allow yourself to examine it closer you see the problem with their discovery. They established a prebiotic atmosphere; we currently live in an oxidizing atmosphere. The atmosphere they created did not have the oxygen to sustain life, and therefore life had to begin in water to get the needed oxygen to live. There are a few problems with this aspect of the experiment, the first being that this prebiotic atmosphere could not sustain any vegetation, which is also living cells. Where did the vegetation come from, and when did the atmosphere make the change to sustain it? Also the idea that life had to start in the water is fallible because water could not sustain the polymerization or the development of single cells. The prebiotic atmosphere was at best simply guessing what might have been because this was the only way to bring about the result they desired. It also defies the second law of thermodynamics, which states that things begin in order but degenerate to chaos. Here we have an echo system beginning in chaos and evolving to order. So this experiment assumed an unscientific atmosphere, and that alone damages any conclusions.

That said, the larger problem lies in what they were able to create in the experiment. The life they created was bacteria, not a cellular organism or simple cell structure, but bacteria. For bacteria to live and grow, it needs a host, or a cellular organism, without which it will die, but this experiment did not produce a cellular organism.

Also something to consider is that a single cell needs several hundred proteins. Where would those proteins come from? How would the cell develop and grow without the building blocks of life? If we could create a primordial goo, as it were, with all the exact amino acids and proteins needed for life, we could still not generate a single cell or sustain it. This brings us back to the question that cannot be answered: where did life come from? Where did life originate?

The DNA-RNA codes in our bodies are so complex they could not be compiled by random mutations. Random implies independent steps, but the steps of DNA-RNA are dependent upon one another. If I may break it down, DNA-RNA are like the ingredients and directions for life. Let's say you are making a cake; DNA would be the ingredients, and RNA would be the directions. They are dependent on one another to be able to get to the end product.

Life and its complexities display the work of a designer. There are questions that cannot be answered by the Big Bang or evolution but would appear to come in line with the claims of the Bible.

So what do evolutionists really say? Evolutionist Paul Davies says, "No one really knows how a mixture of lifeless chemicals spontaneously organized themselves into the first living cell." Evolutionist and biochemist Franklin Herald wrote, "We must concede that there are presently no detailed Darwinian accounts of the evolution of any biochemical or cellular system, only a variety of wishful speculation." The one that pertains most to the theme of this book comes from Francis Crick, the co-discoverer of the double helix structure of DNA. He wrote, "Biologists must constantly keep in mind that what they see was not designed but rather evolved." I have to keep telling myself that even if what I see shows advanced engineering and design, I am not allowed to consider this as a possibility. This is where so many live, bound to something that doesn't hold water, so to speak. While if there is a possible answer, and it makes sense, we cannot consider it if it points to God. As I pointed out in the previous chapter, this debate truly isn't academic or intellectual in nature; it is spiritual.

Darwin himself, in chapter 14 of his book *Origin of Species*, states, "Evolution assumes a being with reproductive powers, and offers no answer for its source since DNA is so complex." Some of the other flaws in the theory of evolution are the origin of feelings, emotions, and morality. There are just no viable answers with the Big Bang or the evolutionary theory.

So assuming we can overcome this and say that life just happened somehow, would evolution then make sense? Could it be more than just a theory? It is taught very often as a matter of science, but science is not supposed to be based solely on theory. Yet there are no fossil records to back up evolution. Even the erroneous theory that Neanderthals represented a gorilla-like off shoot in the chain of modern humans is not sound. It was first proposed between 1911 and 1913 but was completely refuted later, yet it still remains a teaching of "science." True science should embrace truth, not be afraid that truth might reveal something damaging to someone's point of view.

Dr. Colin Patterson, senior paleontologist at the British Museum of Natural History, was quoted as saying the following in response to someone questioning why he offered no pictorial evidence of transitional fossils: "I fully agree with your comments on the lack of direct illustration of evolutionary transitions in my book. If I knew of any, fossil or living I would certainly have included them." The truth of the matter is there are no transitional fossils or creatures, leaving evolution an unproven theory at best. Steven Jay Gould, Harvard paleontologist and evolutionist, wrote, "The extreme rarity of transitional forms in the fossil record persists as the trade secret of paleontology." The fossil record we do have shows all species existing at once, which again would fit the Biblical account of creation.

Another quote that needs to be pointed out is the following statement made by Dr. Scott Todd: "Even if all the data points to an intelligent designer, such an hypothesis is excluded from science because it is not naturalistic." We are not allowed to consider it? This does not sound like someone who is free to think but instead is confined to believe what he has been told.

What if these men and women of rich education were allowed to consider God? You see, I am allowed to consider evolution, but it takes too much faith for me to believe in evolution. I have spoken to many people over time who declared they were freethinkers, but too often they refused to consider anything that goes against what they believed to be true, and they built their opinions on what others have said, even if what they have said is in error, or at best cannot be proven. I am not tied to a theory that makes no sense, but I am allowed to consider any theory and any angle. I have found what has the ability to answer these questions, and it is the history recorded in the Bible, which comes from God.

I think the best quote to end on is from an evolutionary science philosopher named Mike Ruse. He said, "Evolution is a religion, this was true of evolution in the beginning, and it is still true today." It is without any evidence, it is without any substance, yet it is fought for vigorously by some. This comes back to my original thought:, it is not an academic debate, it is not an intellectual debate, but it is a spiritual conflict at its very core. There is substance to the Bible—, the authenticity, the accuracy of the prophesies, the historical and archaeological evidences, and

OUR ORIGINS

the corroborating evidence from other works of history. Therefore, it is quite a valid source to look at for truth, including the origin of creation and time.

We should take a closer look at so many other things, like the flood. We have found aquatic animal fossils on mountain sides. The fact that we have fossils of different animals preserved in such a way, as though they were fused into the rock or the sedimentary layers were quickly formed around them, is compelling. Even the way rocks and fossils are dated is flawed at best. Carbon 14 lasts only thousands of years, yet carbon 14 and other tissue are found in fossils that are said to be 70 million years old. Also rocks that were formed in the 1980 eruption of Mount St. Helens have been dated at 2.8 million years old even though we know they are only a few decades old.

Again there are so many more things to be discovered, and remember this book is not about pointing all of these things out and then saying, "Believe me." Instead, the purpose of these writings is for you to look into these matters for yourself and form your opinions instead of clinging to someone else's opinion, and that includes my opinions. Be honest with yourself for a moment: when reading the information in this chapter, how did you feel? Did you feel threatened? Did you get emotional as things were discussed? Those are not rational responses to information, and they may be signs that you aren't truly free to think.

We must disconnect ourselves from any intellectual or academic prejudices or presuppositions so that we are free to think objectively when we uncover data. It is imperative that your mind is free in your personal pursuit for truth. Part of knowing where we are going is knowing where we started. Our origins are important—too important to leave to the opinions of others—and that is why my only goal here is to set people free to think. The truth is out there, and it is liberating when you discover it without presupposition, when you discover it in the objective light in which it dwells.

(All quotes in this chapter were taken from the Institution for creation research website and Facebook page)

Chapter 4
This Is No Culture War

Today we see people who are "digging in their heels" and "holding on to their rights." People are so angry with each other, name calling and affixing accusations to one another, not even concerned with the validity of the accusations. This has all the signs of an all-out war, yet the war we seem to be fighting in society is not the real war. It is simply the distraction from what is really happening to us.

Now I have asserted from the beginning that life is spiritual, and we were created by God with an eternal spirit. I am also convinced that spirit within us does respond to prompts from a spiritual realm. We are at war today in this world, but I submit to you this is not a culture war. It is not a war of ideologies or opinions. It is not a war of rights and freedoms either. We are engaged in spiritual warfare, one that goes beyond our natural realm. It is a war in which the stakes are much higher than just personal rights, freedoms, or ideas.

In a culture war, both sides feel as though the other side is trying to take away their freedom. Both sides feel as though they are under attack, so they become defensive and even go on the offensive in order to protect themselves and their freedom.

Enter spiritual warfare. If you can get your enemies so busy fighting each other that they have no time for you, if you can get them to hurt and tear down each other, then you will be victorious. There is an enemy of your soul at work in the spiritual realm deceiving, crafting, scheming, and desiring to destroy God's creation. When it comes to the target of this enemy, we are all at the top. Because of God's love for us, because we are made in His image, we are the targets of Satan.

So why would the enemy of your soul go to so much trouble to create disharmony and chaos? First off, he is the author of confusion, the father of lies, and the enemy of your soul, so it is in his nature to do such. There are also a few strategic reasons for what we see today. The first is to get the people of God so distracted on so many fronts that they are overwhelmed, to get the church so busy fighting so many little battles that there is no way they can win the war. He wants to get the church so busy that we forget that our greatest power is not "our voice" but is actually prayer. Spiritual wars are fought with spiritual weapons, not earthly ones, but we will come back to this thought about spiritual weapons.

Another reason for all of the effort the enemy puts into what we see is to get the individual fearful and unable to think logically. If we give in to paranoia, we fall prey to the propaganda of Satan that declares, "They will take away your rights; they think they are better than you." We are unable to think logically because we are too busy reacting and not seeing clearly what is really happening. We slowly allow anxiety and fear into our lives—almost completely undetected—until they have taken away our ability to think rationally. The last thing the enemy wants is for you to be free to think.

The church is fighting on the wrong fronts in the wrong ways. The individual is being inundated with fear subconsciously, and people are ultimately turned against each other in a "culture war." The other benefit for the enemy in all of this is the lines are drawn in the sand. "People who don't think like I do are my enemy, and they are trying to take away my freedom. I can't agree with my enemy even if what they are saying seems to be true; they just want to prove me wrong." A big part of the end game is to divide people in a way in which unity is almost impossible, rational thought goes out the window, and people are oblivious to the fact they are being used as puppets in a much larger game. This illustrates exactly what Jesus was saying when He was speaking truth but the people could not receive it. They were blinded to it, enslaved by the enemy of their soul, and they were completely unaware of these facts.

Then comes the camouflage of the enemy. At the onset of this chapter I stated that the eternal spirit within each of us picks up on what is happening in the spiritual realm. We know deep down that something is going on; there is an intentional division happening here. Before we get to the true source of that division, we are diverted by the enemy, and we now have a group of the populace affixing the blame on the government or the media as the responsible party trying to cause division and confusion. Meanwhile, the enemy stays hidden behind other people and accomplishing his purpose of division, confusion, fear, and anger, and people stay trapped in the game he is playing.

In a culture war there needs to be sides, ideas, and philosophies, but we are not disputing ideology or opinion. We are disputing truth; we are disputing the authority of God and His word. Yet very few can actually see that aspect of what is happening because we have been told our rights, freedoms, and liberties are on the line. When we surrender to that, we are no longer allowed to think for ourselves; we are no longer free to think. Considering that we also cannot agree with our enemy, if someone does not think the way I do, then they become my enemy, which leads me to remain faithful to the dogma I hold to even when it is refuted successfully.

So how did we get to where we are today? The truth is it took time and careful planning by the enemy of your soul. It started by deteriorating the first institution God created. You may be thinking I am speaking of the church, but the first institution God created was not the church; it was the family. Within the family each member plays a vital role that supports and builds each other. There is an idea we see in the Bible: if someone wants to rob someone else, they first bind the strong man, and then spoil his house. Remember that Satan is crafty and deceiving, prowling around like a roaring lion, seeking whom he may devour. This is what he set in motion to get us where we are today.

First take dad and mom out of the home, make them so busy that they can neither invest in nor protect their family. Then devalue the role of the father. If he tries to lead or care for his family, he is chauvinistic and out of touch. Then devalue the role of the mother. Raising kids and cooking dinners are things of the past; going to work for someone else instead of investing in your family is a higher calling.

Now before we go too far into this and you start thinking, "This guy is just old fashioned," I want you to consider something. What would make someone hear these thoughts and say, "That is old fashioned"? Would it be a case of classical conditioning? *Classical conditioning* is a psychology term that basically means you have been trained to think this way by situations, surroundings, and experiences. Remember what we are aiming for here. The desire is not to sell morals to you; the desire is to get you to think for yourself, to observe things objectively and step back from everything you have heard before to analyze what you can discover as you search for truth.

Through the course of the last few generations the roles of manhood and being a true father have been mocked and devalued, the same for the role of the mom as a nurturing adult who often shows us how to love in tender ways and how to truly care for others in a nurturing fashion. It really takes both parents investing in each child to give them a strong emotional and psychological foundation to grow into an adult.

So if mom and dad are devalued and removed from the roles they are gifted to perform in, what happens next? The children become vulnerable to attacks of the enemy. You cannot drive down a highway, watch television, use the Internet, or even listen to most music without being flooded by images and thoughts of sex, anger, death, self-centeredness, and evil. Perhaps adults can see such things and can put them in perspective for what they are, but when children are exposed to such things daily with no strong guidance, they begin to develop the thinking that this is just normal behavior because it seems as though everyone is doing it. If the enemy of your soul has successfully bound the strong man—mom and dad—then the next step is to exploit the next generation, indoctrinating them into a way of thinking that is harmful to both them and society.

The enemy has worked so hard to desensitize and harden people that our society has come to a point where people are losing the desire to love. When I say *love*, I mean to truly love. We will get into this topic soon in the chapter 7, but for now we have come to a place where we live in a society of hurt people—people who are afraid to be hurt anymore and so they defend what they have left, or at least that is what they believe they are doing. Thus the idea of war, which some would label as a culture war, but again, I submit to you, this is no culture war.

One of the things in our world today that is damaging us as individuals is abortion. Before you think for a moment we are about to get political in any way, I assure you we will not. I do not believe for a second the answers we need are found in politics, and I especially do not believe any one political party has the solution for our world today. Again, this is no culture war; free your mind for a second and think with me. What was your first instinct when you heard me speak of abortion as a problem? Did you think, "He must be a republican"? Truth be told, I am not. Why would someone's mind make a presupposition of someone based off of one thing they say? It is because we have been classically conditioned to think this way, to label things and to classify things as possible threats or allies. Free yourself from this, and let's reason together about a few of the things we face in today's world.

Let's get back to the topic of abortion. Mother Teresa once said, "If we accept that a mother can kill even her own child, how can we tell other people not to kill one another?" That is a powerful statement, one that may raise different emotions, but remember we are not diving into the emotional here; we simply want to look at the facts of what is happening around us. I am not your enemy, and you are not mine, regardless of how you believe right now. We are just a couple of people looking for truth, looking for what is real, even if it contradicts what we already believe or what we have been told.

I say this carefully, but what brought abortion to the place it is today was based on statements that were untrue. In the case *Roe v. Wade*, it was stated the pregnancy in question was a result of rape. Almost a decade later that story was recanted by the one who told it; she admitted she was not being honest. The doctor in the trial also admitted to making up the statistical numbers he had presented to the court in order to get a favorable outcome. So just looking at this objectively raises a few red flags. Why tell things that weren't true? Why fabricate statistics to achieve an outcome? Something that was built on the premise of deception should be reevaluated.

The deception continues today in practice and in terminology. It continues in practice because most abortion providers do not want the mother to see a sonogram of the infant she is carrying. The reasoning is because once she sees a moving "fetus" she may be moved emotionally and decide against an abortion. Instead mothers have been told that it is a clump of tissue, not yet formed, still becoming a baby, but not yet being a baby. We know that even at eight weeks arms and legs are forming and are visible, but this doesn't change the fact that in the past women have been told that is not true, and even today in some cases these inaccurate statements are still being made. To say that it is not life is an interesting statement. The reason I say that is to "call" a death, one checks for a heartbeat, and when the heartbeat has stopped it is then called a death.

When a heartbeat starts at two to three weeks into a pregnancy, wouldn't it be logical to call that life? If we say death happens at the end of the heart beating, then we are establishing a heartbeat as a sign of life. Again, take any feelings or emotions out of the equation right now and see what just the truth is saying. There are countless firsthand experiences from medical professionals and abortion patients alike that tell horrifying tales of what they have seen and experienced. Again we are just taking into account the truth of what we can observe.

Let's look also at the terminology itself, calling the unborn baby, your future offspring, a fetus. Why call it a fetus? Some say it is a medical term for an undeveloped baby, but the truth is it is a Latin term that means "offspring." We literally say baby in a different language; is it so we don't have to say the word *baby* to a mother who is considering ending the development of the fetus/baby? It is something that deserves consideration and something we need to think about if we are truly free to think for ourselves.

Abortion is indeed an industry of sorts to man, but to the enemy of your soul it is an opportunity to hurt and desensitize people even more. One thing you do not often hear about in abortion is the after effects on the mother. Most will go through depression, mental and emotional anguish, and even physical complications. Women are being told "this is your right, and someone wants to take it away from you." They aren't told that they are not receiving the whole truth and that there is an element of deception in the terminology, the origination of its legalization, and in the practice of abortion. Why is that true? We can see it is true, but why? These are things that merit our scrutiny but can only be analyzed properly by one who has no agenda, political or otherwise—someone who has only an interest in finding the truth about what it really is and then deciding if they are okay with what it really is.

When you consider the procedure of abortion and what exactly is done, than you can know what it truly is. I am not spelling out the procedure here in this book for one reason and one reason only: because I want you to find out for yourself what is done. Then you will know what it really is, and you can decide if you are okay with what it is or not. Not the idea behind it, definitely not the politics behind it, but literally what is done during an abortion. When you uncover that for yourself, make that choice. You owe it to yourself to be informed.

Do you know why we can't often tackle such things as abortion or other tough issues? It is because so many have been convinced they are engaged in a culture war in which someone wants to take away their rights. It is because the enemy of your soul has convinced people it is all about ideas, and because this is war, you cannot agree with your enemy because that would be surrendering your rights. The reason we get so heated on such topics is because we have been trained by the spiritual forces around us to do so, and we have been unaware of that fact because the enemy hides behind the guise of "we cannot consider anything that is not naturalistic." We essentially blind ourselves and hand ourselves over to be slaves when we are not free to think. We see logically what makes sense, but again, we cannot agree with our enemy because this is war. Please understand you cannot have a logical conversation with an irrational person, thus the need to see the spiritual blindness that affects our society.

We are indeed locked in a confrontation in our day, but it is not a war with each other. We are in a conflict that goes much deeper than ideas and ideology. We are in a war, but this is no culture war; this is a spiritual war, and a spiritual war will not be won by using natural means. A spiritual war is fought properly with weapons that are spiritual in nature: prayer, meditation, love. Yes, love is spiritual in nature, and we will look at that soon, but know this: I am not your enemy, and you are not mine. Even if we think completely differently, even if we believe completely differently, that will not make us enemies in the slightest. What it makes us is people capable of coming to our own conclusions and thinking for ourselves. That is what happens when you become free to think.

Chapter 5

The Moral Compass

For ages a compass has been used by explorers, sailors, pilots, travelers, and more to find their way to their destination. When functioning properly, a compass can trace the direction you are heading and get you to the place you are meant to go. When it is not functioning properly, a compass will guide you off course, and you could end up in a completely different place than what you had intended. The truth is it only has to be off by a little to send you on a path that could hold peril and danger that you are not prepared for.

Throughout this book I have expressed my belief that the Bible is the word of God and is the source of truth as given to us by God. In the pages of this book one can find directions for living, physical and emotional health, success, business, and many other principles. In this book's pages we also see the rise and fall of so many civilizations and the pitfalls that lead to their demise. We see the examples of what service is, what love truly is, and how we can love a life of peace and contentment. There is so much contained in the pages of the Bible it would be foolish to attempt to speak of everything contained in it in just one chapter of a book. The point of all of this is that the Bible can serve as our moral compass, our guide in everyday life.

Joshua is told by God to meditate in this book of the law day and night that he may be prosperous and have good success. God encourages Joshua to observe and put into practice everything that is written, not turning to the right or the left. The Bible can be used as a moral compass to take us to our place of destiny in life. It can also be a daily guide to know true success in life.

Through the teachings of the Bible we see the importance of service, humility, forgiveness, and true love for one another. So with such a device at our disposal, how did we get to the place we are as a society? How did we come to a place where people are so angry, discouraged, depressed, and full of fear? Perhaps we forgot that we have a moral compass, or perhaps we have been told it can't be trusted and we just accepted that as truth.

The Bible teaches that love, joy, peace, patience, kindness, goodness, faithfulness, gentleness, and self-control are the fruit of the spirit. What that means is much like a tree produces fruit as a result of what is happening on the inside of that tree, we should produce these fruits in our lives as a result of what is happening inside our spirit. We should display these characteristics not because we are trying to display each one but as a result of the person we are becoming. The Bible shows us how to become that person who has these characteristics, or fruits, in our life.

Instead we have laid aside our moral compass and picked up what is called "subjective truth," or guidelines that can change depending on our circumstances. In doing this we have begun to display a different type of fruit in our world today. We are not displaying love, joy, peace, patience, kindness, goodness, faithfulness, gentleness, and self-control. Instead, the fruit we see around us today is more like hatred, anger, depression, fear, meanness, rudeness, selfishness, abusiveness, and no self-control. Again, what we are displaying is a result of what is happening inside of us. We can take the position that we are simply responding to our situations in our day and age, but deep down we know that is an excuse; we know that is not the truth. Our character should not be given to us by the world around us; it should be developed by something inside of us. It should be developed intentionally as we follow a path that will take us where we want to go, a path we can follow if we have a working moral compass.

So why can't people be free of these things? Why won't people reach for the moral compass that can be found in the words of God? It is because of the same underlying problem that has been addressed throughout this book: the lies of the enemy of your soul. "God's rules are so restrictive; He doesn't want you to have fun or to feel good. His law holds you in back experiencing life; this is a cage God wants to put you in, and you aren't allowed to have fun."

These are all lies that Satan whispers to our spirit. If we aren't free to think for ourselves, we accept those lies, and we become prisoners under the guise of freedom. We become our own jailer. We have the key to freedom; we just aren't allowed to consider it if we are bound up in the lies of the enemy of our soul. One by one, people are lead off by Satan into captivity, promised a freedom, promised an enlightenment, but given only a death sentence and blinded to the very truth that can set them free.

You cannot and you should not ever try to argue someone out of this kind of prison. It will accomplish nothing. It will instead draw the divide even deeper between people and make Satan's hold stronger over them. The information in this book—and all of the information available to you that I hope you will begin to look at—is never meant to be ammunition for arguments. It is meant to open your eyes, build your faith, and allow you to be free to think for yourself. This is something we need to get a firm grasp on because what we are motivated by is very much a part of the moral compass that guides our lives. We should be motivated by truth and love.

So why is it so hard for people to get free once this has happened? Why can't people just return to the moral compass? It makes sense if it brings peace, love, joy and so many other good things to our lives. The reason is the same reason the people in John 8 could not receive what Jesus was saying: they had been spiritually blinded to the truth. Now they are sold the lie, you are free, and you are in a culture war in which your enemy wants to take your freedom. We already addressed the craftiness of this plan: if I feel I am at war I have to defend myself, and I cannot agree with my enemy, even if he is right. We are not each others' enemies; we are all part of the creation of God almighty.

The further we go without a moral compass (or following an incorrect guide), the further we get from where we are supposed to be and the more likely we are to fall into snares and dangers. In just a few generations we have gone from a time when the president would get on the air and lead an entire nation in prayer to a time where teachers, coaches, and even students can be sued for praying. You may be thinking, "Come on, that's not true, that doesn't happen." The truth is it happens a lot.

Coach Joe Kennedy lost his job for his actions, and then the Ninth Circuit Court of San Francisco ruled in favor of the ACLU who had sued the coach for his actions. Now what did this coach do? Surely he was handing out religious material or trying to get his players to believe the way he believed, right? Nope, that wasn't it. So maybe he was forcing them to pray with him, right? No, his defiant action was at the end of each game, after shaking hands with the other coach and team, he would take a knee and silently thank God for protecting everyone from injury and for a great time that day. The prayer wasn't out loud, and no one was asked or even encouraged to join in. The lawsuit stated people could see him take a knee and that could not be tolerated.

From a president leading a nation vocally in prayer to a coach who is no longer allowed to silently take a knee, we have degenerated into a realm of not allowing people to be free to think for themselves. I wish this was an anomaly, but truthfully there are so many cases just like this one in our court systems today. If we don't course correct, where will we be in the next generation? We can expose our kids to sex, murder, anger, violence, and more, but we cannot tolerate young people being exposed to someone praying. This is where I ask you to please set aside political or ideological prejudices and just think with me for a moment. Do you see an issue with the last statement? Do you see an issue with what today's world is okay and not okay with exposing our young people to? We are not in a culture war, I assure you, and the only way out of where we are is to be able to think for yourself and not the way society, or more accurately the spiritual force behind society, is leading you to think.

Let's look at the story of Masterpiece Cake Shop. They politely said they would not bake a wedding cake for two men celebrating a same-sex marriage. They were not rude, and they were apologetic, but they were simply expressing their moral convictions. The two men, with the help of the ACLU, filed suit, and the bakery has stopped making wedding cakes instead of following the court directive to make wedding cakes celebrating same-sex marriages, which has cost them approximately 40 percent of their business while they appeal the decision. Why? Because they politely declined to make a cake that went against their beliefs. Take that statement into account when you think about this. They are being sued, they may lose their life's work, their business, and people are yelling all manner of foul words at them and saying they are full of hate. This is one of those moments I really need you to remove your prejudices again and simply think about this. First, is it fair that they lose everything because they have a moral conviction about baking a cake? Second, do you see the irony of them being called names and being threatened and being told they are full of hate? Logic tells us that doesn't make sense at all, but emotion drives us to pick a side and fight. What are you driven by? Are you getting free to think yet?

I wish this was a single incident, but again there are many other cases just like this right now. What is happening is there are those in places of power who are saying, "We will tell you what you can say yes and no to." That does not sound like someone who is free to think; that sounds like someone who is afraid of those who are free to think. This is about conformity: "You must accept what I believe in or I can sue you, and I can force you to accept my beliefs." Logically speaking, we know we can disagree with each other and still be friends, but that destroys the plans of the enemy of your soul.

We must remember that our war is not natural; it is not with people. It is with the one who is lying to them and holding them captive so they cannot receive the truth. You cannot have a rational conversation with an irrational person, but remember, that doesn't make us each others' enemies. The moral compass we have been talking about, the Bible, teaches us to pray for those who harm us, bless those who persecute us, and to bless and not curse. What if we all lived by such a moral guide, one where we didn't seek revenge or justification, but instead we sought peace, even if it meant humbling ourselves?

I understand there is actually a "hate" list, a list of companies or organizations that value traditional marriage and do not believe in gay marriage. Again, please see this for what it is. People are convinced there is a culture war and that their rights are under attack, so they are defending them and identifying their enemy. Let's look at this logically for a moment. No one has ever accused me of hating thieves even though I believe theft is wrong. No one has ever accused me of hating people who take God's name in vain or even hating murderers. The reason is because logically it wouldn't make sense to do so, but when we are driven by emotion and irrational thought, anything goes. The idea is to be free to see things for what they are, to be able to think for ourselves. If we do not once again grasp the moral compass that can lead us to truth, we may never know true freedom ever again. Instead, we will remain slaves to pleasure and selfish desire, never truly understanding love and never truly being free to think.

Chapter 6

The New Moral Compass

In our day we have a new moral compass that doesn't operate on the premise of a true north. It doesn't operate with a consistent point of reference. Instead it is ever changing and taking us different directions, often times frustrating us. You see, when you alter a compass you end up in a place you may never have intended to go, even a place you may not necessarily want to be. The same remains true with the moral compass we trust to guide us. If we alter it or replace it with one that doesn't operate the same, we may find ourselves in a place we were never intended to be.

What once was considered embarrassing, rude, perverse, or just plain wrong is now celebrated as liberating thought and enlightened. Many say we are at a new age of enlightenment, but we have become more shallow than ever in the way we live, the way we believe, and definitely in the way we think.

Today we look to entertainment for our guiding principles. Morally bankrupt individuals are being propped up by Satan to spread his propaganda, to be ambassadors of culture, but what they are spreading is anger and hatred, calling good, evil, and calling evil, good. With the role of mom and dad diminished in our society, we are seeing a generation being indoctrinated with ideas that are called truth.

The new moral compass is one that allows people to declare others full of hate while they are using every hurtful word they can think of to describe them. It is a compass that allows people to say, "I am all about love and tolerance," but then wish death on someone. It allows people to say they are full of acceptance and then wish ill on someone's wife or children without a second thought. The new moral compass will twist a person until they do not know which way is up and they are not who they want to be. It will take you to a place of irrational thought, thus confusing you and trapping you, not allowing you to see the direction you truly want to go. It takes you to a place where you can no longer think for yourself but instead must conform to those around you.

The new moral compass says if most people are doing it and it feels good, then it should be okay because the end justifies the means. That is a familiar-sounding thought, and it is so very prevalent in today's society. This is the logic of a society that is lost and doesn't have a true moral compass that can get them to where they truly want to go. We don't want to hear a truth of morals, and certainly not of God, or of accountability. Therefore we reject any truth that points to God in any way—the truth about the Bible, the truth about our origins, even the truth about our future—because what we really want is to feel good right now. We forgo our future in favor of our current desire or pleasure. The truth is "right now" screams louder, but "later" lasts longer.

Let me run this thought by you: I don't want to be comfortably sick. I want to be well. If you give me an aspirin for a headache and the pain goes away, then I get better. Great. If the headache is caused by a tumor, though, and you give me an aspirin so I can be comfortable but you do nothing about the tumor, you really haven't helped me at all. The idea of the temporal feel-good lifestyle comes at a price that is paid later and possibly even for eternity. I don't want to be comfortably sick. We have a society that could see a cure in the truth of God for what we are going through today, but it might take away the momentary pleasures, so we ignore the cure because we are blinded to our own futures. This is what happens when we don't replace our broken moral compass but instead complain about the things that point out we are in the wrong place. We treat the symptom but never the real problem, and we remain lost.

As we can see, the moral compass of this world points only to here and now; it gives no direction for the future. Therefore it becomes easy for us to trade what we want most for what we want right now. We have lost our way as a society, but it is never too late to correct the path. It is never too late to grab the moral compass of God's word and get on track once again.

The word of God is the standard, the truth, and the moral compass. It can lead us to a prosperous and healthy lifestyle and community. The enemy of your soul has fought hard to get it removed, to discredit it, but the light always overcomes the darkness. The enemy of your soul generates a spiritual blindness to stop eyes from being opened to the truth, but I know the one Who opens blinded eyes. I know the one Who has the truth that sets people free. He is the one who is calling you to be free to think.

Chapter 7
The Truth About Love

How important is love? This is a question we need to answer for ourselves. As we are contemplating that question, here is one of even greater significance. Do we know what love is?

We will come back to the second one soon. First off, how important is love? In 1 Corinthians 13, the apostle Paul considers a few scenarios such as sacrificing himself, giving away everything he has, and doing great works, and says he can do all of this, but if he doesn't love, he has done nothing but make some noise. In Mark 12:30, Jesus is asked what the greatest commandment is. He responds by saying, "Love the Lord your God with all your heart, with all your soul, with all of your mind, and with all your strength." He then went on to say, "The second is this: 'Love your neighbor as yourself.' There is no commandment greater than these" (Mark 12:31).

He says that all of the law, all of the commandments, and all of the prophets hang on these two commandments, that love is the fulfillment of the law. In Romans 13, we see again that love is the fulfillment of the law and that he who loves his neighbor has fulfilled the law. In the book of 1 John 3, we read, "He who does not love his brother or fellow man abides in death." In John 13, Jesus says, "By this shall all men know you are my disciples if you have love one for another." Finally, in John 15, Jesus says, "This is my command: love one another as I have loved you."

It seems that love is not only important, but it is vital, absolutely crucial to life itself. So we know the importance of love, and we can grasp its magnitude and proper place in who we are and how we live, but do we know what love is? You might think that a silly question, but the majority of the population today does not truly know what love is. One of the main reasons is much like truth (and life): love finds its origins in God Himself.

> Love is patient, love is kind, it does not envy, and it does not boast. Love is not proud, it never dishonors others, it is not self-seeking, and it is not easily angered. Love keeps no record of wrongs, it does not delight in evil, but it rejoices in truth. Love always protects, always trusts,

always hopes, always perseveres, and love never fails. (1 Cor. 13:4–8

Let that sink in for a moment and see if it lines up with your definition of love. Do you think the culture around us feels this way about love? Or does the culture have an inaccurate view of what love really is.

We live in a day where, through so many different avenues, a distorted view of love is presented to us and especially to the young people to the point that people see love as being subjective, just like most truth that is held to. The prevailing thought is love expresses itself in the physical, but in truth that is not accurate. Love expresses itself emotionally, mentally, and spiritually, but it spends itself physically.

The reason we have a distorted or inaccurate view of what love is, is because we have morally and spiritually bankrupt individuals trying to redefine a moral and spiritual truth. Just like with life, truth, morality, and ethics, love also finds its origin in and from God. Just like with truth, morality, and ethics, the enemy of your soul desires to twist love and pervert it into something entirely different so that you and I would never know what it really could be like.

Here is a question we need to consider: can you love someone and not have sex with them? In like manner, can you have sex with someone and not love them? I am thinking the obvious answer to both questions is yes, but things are not always as obvious as they should be in our world today. I once shared online with someone who was a proponent of casual sex both heterosexual and homosexual sex, that I love many people but I am not drawn to have sex with them. Then I stated I have only ever had sex with one person in my entire life, and that is my wife. They responded, "I can't possibly wrap my head around your idea of love." To them, love was not patient, kind, or anything else the Bible says. To them, love was gratification and pleasure. So many people struggle with relationships today because they struggle with the true identity of what love is. We equate love and sex like one equals the other, but we already know you can have one without the other from the question we just looked at a moment ago.

The Bible has many examples of what love looks like. Take the example of Ruth and Naomi. Ruth left her homeland and went to care for Naomi. She loved her, lived with her, and they cared for each other, and this is a picture of love. There were no sexual desires or need for sexual pleasures to be fulfilled. Instead, they enjoyed a mutual love that few in this day truly understand and some may never even know.

We can also reference the example of David and Jonathan. The Bible says they loved each other. In fact, the Bible says Jonathan loved David as his own flesh, and they embraced one another, looked out for one another, even cried over one another. This is a picture of what love truly is. It is not about sex or even infatuation; it is something much deeper than that. Love is a deep spiritual bond and not just a cheap thrill. At one point many years later when David became king, he searched for anyone who was still alive and related in any way to Jonathan so he could show kindness to them in honor of his bond with Jonathan. David found a descendant who was lame and brought him into the king's palace to live in response to his deep love for and commitment to Jonathan. Again, this is a relationship that defies today's understanding of love in so many ways.

The truth is because of our misunderstanding of what love is we automatically think taking our relationship to the next level means sex. Maybe you have seen that interpretation before in stories, television, or movies. We have been trained to think this way by our surroundings—not because of a culture war but because the enemy of your soul does not want you to experience how real love can affect you in such a deep and meaningful way.

There are a few different types of love the Bible talks about, the first of which is *agape* love. This is the foundation of all love. It is sacrificial in nature, unconditional, selfless, and eternal. People say they understand love, but often we go from one emotional high to the next. This process does little more than gratify one's self. It does little for others, yet agape love puts others first and does not think of personal pleasures at all. That is why it is the foundation of any love: it is what love is all about.

There is also *phileo* love. This is a brotherly love and also where we get the name for the city Philadelphia, also called the city of brotherly love. Phileo love is when we love our neighbor, when we have a friendly love for everyone, even those we haven't met yet. This is a friendship or brotherly bond, and again it is rooted in agape love. It is not conditional; it is a fellowship kind of love that is often interactive, involving doing things together or just talking and hanging out.

We also have what is called *storge* love. This is a natural family bond, a love that comes without coercion, a natural love between a parent and a child. This love is just a natural, involuntary response that is displayed in the family.

Finally we have *eros* love, which is where we get the word *erotic*. Now, you may think, "Well, that's it, that's where the world tends to linger." The truth is while sex has become commonplace, that does not mean the world understands eros love. On the contrary, eros love is so much more than just sex; it is everything about the romantic love between a husband and a wife. It is something that is unique and best enjoyed for what it is: a rare, once-in-a-lifetime bond between a husband and wife.

Before we go further on this topic, I want to tell you a little history about the pineapple. Okay this seems a little (or even a lot) off topic, but I promise we are going somewhere here. When settlers from Europe came to America, they found something they had never seen before. It was hard on the outside like a pinecone and sweet on the inside like an apple. They had never seen anything like it before and didn't know what to think of it. They took some back to their homeland with them, and these rare items they came to call pineapples were sold for what today would be the equivalent of $1,200 each. Now the story takes an unexpected turn. The people who bought the pineapples wouldn't actually eat them. Instead, they would set them on a table and cover them with a cloth. Then they would invite people over to a viewing party where they would uncover the pineapple and display it because it was so rare and precious. Only the wealthiest people could own a pineapple.

Obviously this is not the case any longer. Pineapples are now sold for much less. Why? Because they became so readily available to everyone and were no longer rare or special. The value it had was found in its rarity, in its uniqueness. This is no different than erotic, or romantic, love. Romantic love is meant to be special, unique, and rare, but when it becomes just another common thing, we miss the true pleasure of what it was designed to be, and we rob ourselves of a once-in-a-lifetime opportunity.

What if the world around us really got the full impact of what love truly is? How differently would we treat each other? In order for this to happen, people have to be free to think, to see for themselves what love really is and be allowed to accept that truth really can find its roots in God. Instead, people are being led by the lies of the enemy of their soul, only to be hurt, unfulfilled, and ultimately without hope, which is the end game of the enemy. All the while Satan simply laughs at his success, and our pain.

I can't and I won't try to redefine love or marriage; it is not something I have the ability to do. It is something established by God and not by man. It is something that was created by God and not by man. That said, I love homosexuals, I love lesbians, I love transgenders, and do you know why? Because of Jonah 4:11. This is where God is reasoning with Jonah about the people in Ninevah. They did things that were wrong. they did things that were evil, and Jonah didn't care for them at all; he had no compassion for them. Then God illustrated something for Jonah. He caused a vine to grow and give Jonah shade from the heat, then he also caused the same vine to wither and die. Jonah cared for that vine because it made him feel better; it shaded him from the heat. God then challenged Jonah (paraphrased): "You did not plant it or care for it, it sprung up overnight, and died overnight, and yet you cared for it."

THE TRUTH ABOUT LOVE

Jonah replied that he did care for it. Then God said to Jonah (paraphrased), "There are 120,000 people in Ninevah who don't know their right hand from their left. Don't I have the right to care for them?" Yes, they were lost, and yes, they did evil things, but God still loved them, just as he loves each of us.

I love the book of Jonah because it is the only book in the Bible that ends with a question. I believe that question is valid to us today. Think of someone whom you just cannot be around. Think of a person that just gets under your skin and is even down right mean to you, then ponder that last line from the book of Jonah where God says, "Don't I have a right to love them?" If you are a Christian, you not only have the right but the duty to love them regardless of what they have done because God has done even more for each of us. He has forgiven each of us more than we will ever be able to forgive someone else, so who are we to respond in any other way except forgiveness and love?

Only the supernatural love of God can change a heart. This book was never meant to take a platform of "us verse them" but instead to point out practical facts and truths, at least enough to get you to investigate them for yourself so that you can become free to think. The next chapter might be the toughest one for my Christian readers to handle, but we all need to be free to think, and that is what we will attempt to do one more time in chapter 8.

Chapter 8
We Are as Close to God as We Want to Be

*T*hat's an interesting title for a chapter, but honestly, it is completely accurate. Ultimately, no one can keep you from God. No situation, not even your schedule can keep you from God. No outside interference or circumstances can invade or interrupt your relationship with God. The only thing that can possibly do that is you. You see, we cannot control everything that happens to us. In the grand scheme of things, life will throw curveballs; it will even knock you down at times. There will be times when it seems life is just not fair, but even in light of all of this—all of the things we cannot control—we still are in charge of our responses, our actions, and our decisions. We decide when we stop; no one else can do that. They can try to hinder us, and they can slow us down, but no one can ever stop us from being closer to God. That is simply a choice each of us must make for for ourselves.

When Jesus came He taught the understanding that God desires a relationship with His creation. While Jesus taught this truth, He did not introduce this truth. In fact, this truth was introduced when God created man. If you want to know what God's plan is, you need to look no further than the first few chapters of Genesis. We were created for fellowship with our Creator. Then man sinned, disobeyed, and broke that fellowship, and God has been restoring that fellowship ever since. Ultimately we will be restored to that fellowship once again, and the reason we will is because of the sacrifice of Jesus Christ taking away the sin debt we could not pay so we can once again be restored to fellowship with God. It is sin that entered into the world through the act of man that separated us from God, and it is still something that can affect us to this day, but it doesn't have to any longer.

In Hebrews 12, we are encouraged to throw off every weight and every hindrance and run the race that is set before us, fixing our eyes on Jesus, the author and finisher of our faith, and neglecting everything else that desires our attention and running with perseverance. It requires effort on our part to follow Jesus. Salvation is indeed a free gift, but it is not cheap. It cost Him everything.

We will at times have to fight to overcome the attraction of sin, but we must fight with all of our strength, understanding it is sin that separates us from God.

Sometimes we have the mindset that we have prayed a prayer and now God's hands are tied and He has to let us into Heaven. Understand that you will never earn your way into God's grace. Instead, the things we do are the "fruit," or the product of what is happening inside of us being displayed on the outside through our actions. That said and with the understanding that sin separates us from God, I make the following statement: the extent to which we tolerate known sin in our lives is the extent to which we separate ourselves from God. The truth is we are as close to God as we want to be. We need to know what can hinder us in our walk and development, and that is sin. Therefore, we must learn to throw aside every hindrance and the sin that so easily besets us and run in a way we have never run before.

The other thing that can stop us is unbelief. Why do most people not pray? Is it because we don't have much time? Is it because we are so busy and have so much to do that we just can't? Or is it because we don't believe it will change things? Well, let's look at a scenario and see what the right answer is.

You just got home from work, the kids need help with homework, you have to make dinner, the house is a mess, and you have a headache. We have all seen this play out at least once; some of us even see this once a week. Suddenly the phone rings, and you have the opportunity to claim one million dollars in cash, but there is a catch: the cash is thirty minutes away, and they say you have exactly thirty-four minutes to get there. The kids have homework, everyone is tired, cranky, and hungry, you have a headache, and the house is a mess. You hang up the phone; what happens next? If you are like almost anyone else, you drop everything and drive fast, you collect that one million dollars, and you celebrate the victory you have just won.

What does that have to do with prayer? Well, why were you able to drop everything and make a mad dash for thirty minutes to grab one million dollars? Was it because you believed that one million dollars could change your life? It is okay to admit it. We believe one million dollars can change our lives. So why is it so hard to drop everything and pray for thirty minutes? Maybe it's because we don't necessarily believe that prayer will change our lives. Now, we would never audibly say, "I don't believe in prayer," but we often say it by our actions. Sin and unbelief are the biggest stumbling blocks we face. The way to overcome unbelief is with truth and experience, and the way to overcome sin is very much the same.

The matter of salvation in the life of the believer is no small matter, and neither is it something we can address once and never regard it again. We see in Phillippians 2:12 the charge to "continue to work out your own salvation with fear and trembling." Again, understand that salvation is the free eternal gift from

God and that you will never earn it. It is literally a gift that when applied to the life of a believer makes a dramatic, even radical change—a change in the way we live, behave, speak, and the way we think.

We had to get to that part. This book is all about getting you to think, and nothing can clear your mind to thinking freely like connecting to the maker of Heaven and Earth, He who is the source of life, truth, love, and thought.

One well-known preacher Chuck Swindoll once said his seminary professor addressed the graduating class by saying the following: "I fear you may graduate with too many beliefs but not enough convictions." A strong statement, but one that holds very true of many who claim the title "Christian" today. Belief is one thing, but conviction is where belief is put into practice and put into action. Too many today have a lackadaisical approach to faith. The truth is we need to put effort into our faith, and a great place to start is knowing what we believe and why we believe it. I cannot tell you how many people who claim the title "Christian" who have never read the entire Bible. If we are to be truly free to think, then that is something that applies across the board, including in our faith. We must be convinced of the truths we hold to not because someone told us but because we know for ourselves.

When it comes to spiritual growth, it is not a passive thing, but instead it requires great effort and discipline.

Some today will say, "I am spiritual," but they really aren't sure what they believe or, for that matter, what makes them "spiritual." The idea of being free to think is freeing ourselves to look for truth. The reason I say this book was not written to try to convert people to Christianity but to get people to think for themselves is because the truth is out there. I firmly believe if you allow yourself to look at all of the evidence, all of the facts, and to do so objectively, you will find the truth that is out there. The idea is to say, "Go, look for yourself," because the truth is very plainly seen if you will set aside every presupposition and look objectively.

Another thing to consider is that just like every other topic we talked about in this book, you cannot build your view solely on what someone else says. That said, it is good to seek wisdom, and it is okay to inquire of others in the search for truth, but ultimately it is personal discovery that makes it so exciting and helps to establish truth as a foundation as we build our lives. Therefore, we owe it to ourselves to dig deep and never stop learning and growing.

We need authentic truth coming from those who have been grounded in the truth, but that is not what we always get today. A lawyer speaking on the radio recently said law students today no longer study the Constitution, the Declaration of Independence, or any other historical documents. Instead we have a generation of lawyers studying books about these documents, books containing someone else's opinions about these documents. Now, while that is a scary truth, the same can be said for some seminaries today. Many of the upcoming teachers and ministers who will be at the helm of the church are no longer studying the Bible. Instead they are studying books about the Bible. They are studying someone else's opinion about the Bible instead of receiving truth from the source and studying for themselves. Now there are some great companion books to the Bible—history books, geography books, lexicons, even commentaries—but none of these were ever meant to take the place of the Bible.

When we build our truth on someone else's opinions, we risk building our truth on faulty information. Much like with many of the other issues we touched on throughout our time together in this book, if we do not research what we are told, just accepting it as truth, and if it then turns out to be inaccurate, what have we really gained? What should our reaction be? Too often our reaction is to get defensive and stand behind what we have been told instead of discovering solid, life-changing truth.

If we take a lackadaisical approach to our walk with God, we are truly going to miss out. It is a daily development, and when we decide we are tired of pursuing truth, then we have decided "this is as close as I want to get," thus bringing us right back to the thought of this particular chapter: we are as close to God as we want to be.

A statement I have heard many times in my life is "success leaves clues." It is a true statement and one we can witness in many areas of life and faith. If we see the way the disciples walked with Jesus and if we see the way people throughout the Bible were connected to God in such deep relationships, we can see what we should do to have the same results. What did they do? They spent time in the presence of God. They spent time in prayer and in service to God. They didn't rest their entire walk simply on what someone else said; they chased God. Are we chasing God today?

There are two questions that Christians must consider if we are to move forward in faith. What does the world see when they see you and when they see the church? When was the last time the world said, "Thank God for the church"? The Bible makes it clear as we love and as we shine the light that the world will see the good deeds and praise the Father in Heaven. So does the world see the love of Christ when they see us? Does the world around us see our good deeds and praise our Father in Heaven? Those are two sobering questions but ones we must answer if we want to move forward.

The truth is the closer we are to Christ, the more we take on His character. Attributes like love, humility, service, and self-sacrifice for the good of others become the "fruit" we display in our lives as a product of what is happening on the inside. If we aren't displaying these characteristics—if we aren't displaying the spiritual fruit—then we are not as close to God as we could be or should be. We are as close to God as we want to be because we decide when we keep going forward and when we stop.

What does the world see when they see the church? There was a point in the book of Corinthians where Paul was disappointed in the church for taking one another to court. He told them it would be better to be wronged than to damage the witness of the church. He said if we couldn't settle these things within the church, how would we ever reach the destiny God has set before us? Now, before you think we have gotten beyond that in this day and age, I submit to you we have not, and our witness to those around us is not what it should be on a collective level. The best way to change that is one person at a time. If each of us commits to become more Christ-like, or more Christian, then slowly others will see the change and want it as well. Then slowly the face of the church can change, and we can point to the light much more effectively.

Together we have traversed through many topics and covered much ground. There is a lot of truth out there waiting to be discovered. It all starts for you when you set aside presuppositions and objectively dive into the truth that awaits you. The important thing to learn is we are not each others' enemies even if we think differently from one another, but there is an enemy of our souls who desires to see us confused and uninformed. We were each created as spiritual beings, and we find our origin in the Creator of all things. In Him we find truth, love, morals, and meaning. The only thing that can blind us is a desire to not be able to see the truth. It is my prayer that in our time together, you have been given the desire to be free to think.

www.ingramcontent.com/pod-product-compliance
Ingram Content Group UK Ltd.
Pitfield, Milton Keynes, MK11 3LW, UK
UKHW041948230426
12048UKWH00008B/199